My Favorite Pet

RABBIT

Jared Siemens

AV2
www.av2books.com

Step 1
Go to **www.av2books.com**

Step 2
Enter this unique code
SHRTCRGBQ

Step 3
Explore your interactive eBook!

AV2 is optimized for use on any device

Your interactive eBook comes with...

Contents
Browse a live contents page to easily navigate through resources

Audio
Listen to sections of the book read aloud

Videos
Watch informative video clips

Weblinks
Gain additional information for research

Try This!
Complete activities and hands-on experiments

Key Words
Study vocabulary, and complete a matching word activity

Quizzes
Test your knowledge

Slideshows
View images and captions

This title is part of our AV2 digital subscription

1-Year Grades K–5 Subscription ISBN
978-1-7911-3320-7

Access hundreds of AV2 titles with our digital subscription.
Sign up for a FREE trial at **www.av2books.com/trial**

RABBIT

CONTENTS

A Pet Rabbit

People have been keeping rabbits as pets since the 1800s. Rabbits make great pets because they are clean, smart, and quiet. They can also learn to get along with other pets, including dogs and cats.

Rabbits are known for their large ears, which help to **regulate** their body temperatures. Pet rabbits can live to be more than 10 years old. There are more than 3 million pet rabbits in the United States.

Male rabbits are called **bucks**, and **female rabbits** are called **does**.

Life Cycle of a Rabbit

Newborns
Rabbits are born without any fur.

Two to Five Weeks
Baby rabbits come out of their nest to explore.

Eight to Ten Weeks
Young rabbits are ready to stop drinking their mothers' milk.

Six Months
Most rabbits are fully grown and ready to reproduce.

Nose

Rabbits have a strong sense of smell. This is because their noses contain millions of scent **receptors** that detect odors.

A Rabbit's Body

All rabbits have short tails, long ears, and delicate skeletons. The cottontail and domestic rabbit are two of the most common rabbit species in North America.

Legs

A rabbit's **hind legs** are longer than its front legs. When it runs, its hind legs touch the ground first.

Ears

Rabbits do not have sweat glands. Instead, they have blood vessels in their ears that keep their bodies cool.

Eyes

Rabbits have three eyelids. They use their third eyelid to protect their eyes from dust or other **hazards**.

Whiskers

Rabbits have very long whiskers on their faces. They use them to feel their way around in dark places.

Paws

Unlike a cat or a dog, a rabbit does not have protective pads on its paws. Instead, it only has fur for protection.

Choosing a Rabbit

There are more than 60 **breeds** of domestic rabbit. These rabbits range in size from 2 to 13 pounds (1 to 6 kilograms). Before choosing your rabbit, it is important to research the needs and **temperaments** of each breed to find a pet rabbit that will best suit your family.

While Netherland dwarfs are not suitable for small children, Dutch rabbits enjoy cuddling and handling.

Dutch rabbits are **one of the most popular** rabbit breeds.

Rabbit Hutch

Although many people choose to keep their pet rabbits indoors in cages, others house their rabbits outside in wooden hutches. Wooden hutches should be watertight and insulated to keep rabbits safe from weather conditions.

Whether your rabbit lives inside or outside, its home should be a minimum of five times its size. The bottom of a cage should be made of solid material and lined with straw, hay, or aspen shavings.

It is best to place a rabbit's cage or hutch **away from loud noises** and activity.

Healthy Teeth

Rabbits need to chew things. They keep their teeth from growing too long by gnawing on wooden toys and timothy hay. Rabbits have a total of 6 **incisors**, or front teeth, and 22 **molars**.

Pet rabbits should be monitored closely if allowed to roam around your home. Be sure to keep your rabbit away from electrical cords, houseplants, and small objects that could be **ingested**.

Rabbit Fact

A rabbit's front teeth **never stop growing**.

Rabbit Food Pyramid
5%
Healthy Treats
5%
Pellets
10%
Leafy Greens
80%
Hay or Fresh Grass

Rabbit Food

Rabbits are herbivores, which means they eat only plant matter. Their meals consist of hay, fresh grass, rabbit pellets, and fresh leafy greens. Hay is an important part of rabbit diets, as it helps with their digestion.

Although rabbits are often depicted eating carrots in books and on television programs, carrots are too starchy to be the basis of a rabbit's diet. A **veterinarian** can help determine the ideal diet for your particular rabbit.

Rabbits like to have a routine. **Feed your rabbit at the same time** each day.

Rest and Exercise

Rabbits tend to sleep most of the day and night. For this reason, it is important to place a small cardboard box or other shelter in your rabbit's cage or hutch that it can use to hide or sleep.

Rabbits are most active at dawn and dusk. A rabbit needs two or three hours of daily exercise outside its cage or hutch. Rabbits have powerful hind legs made for running and jumping. They can run up to 35 miles per hour (56 kilometers per hour) in short bursts.

Rabbit Fact

Rabbits can jump about **3 feet** (0.9 meters) high.

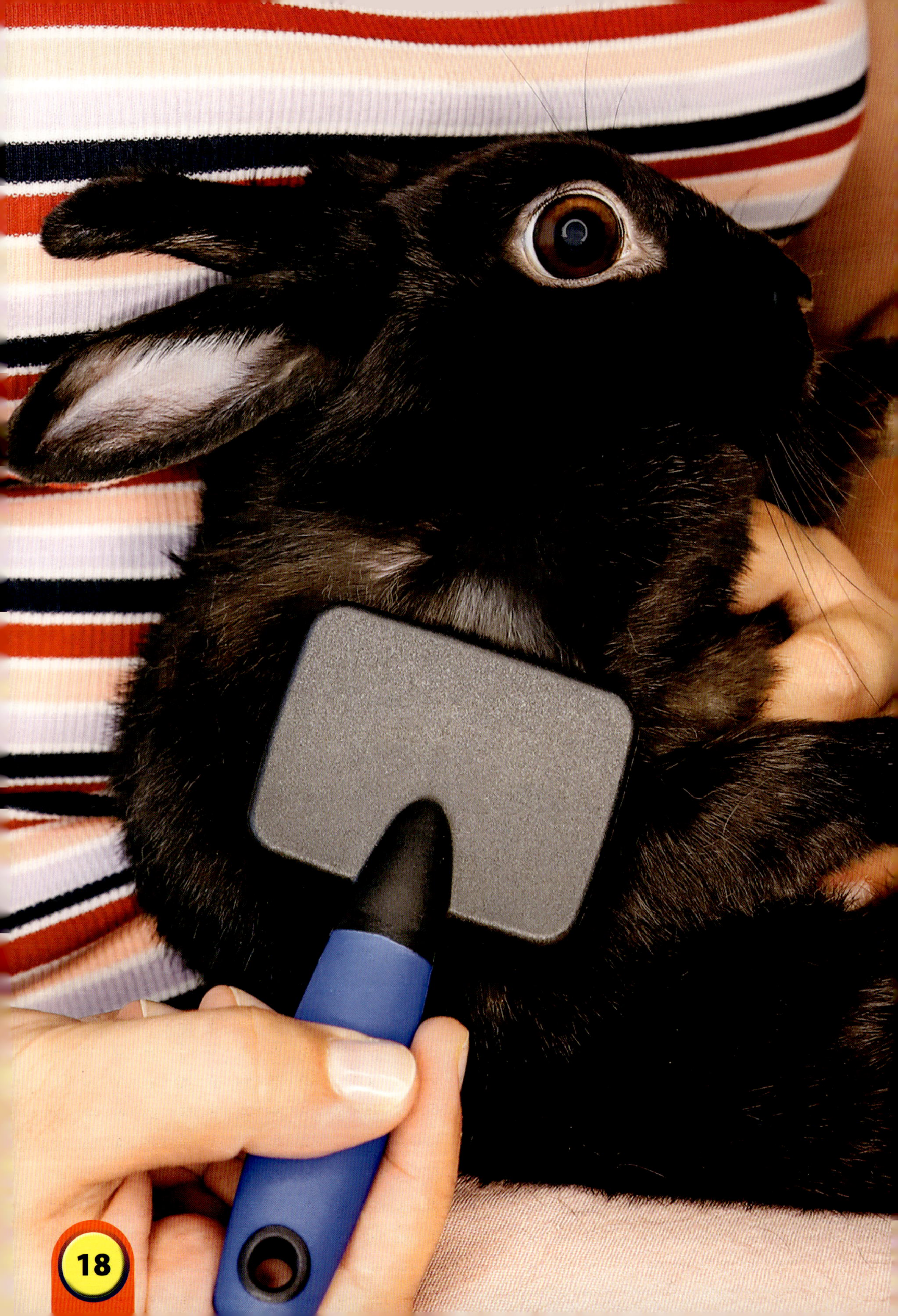

Rabbit Grooming

Rabbits groom themselves like cats, and do not need to be bathed. Bathing a rabbit can be very harmful to its health. If your rabbit has longer fur, it will need to be brushed often to prevent its fur from matting. This will also stop the rabbit from getting hairballs. Hairballs develop when a rabbit swallows too much of its own fur while grooming itself.

Rabbits also need their ears cleaned and nails trimmed on a regular basis.

Rabbits are usually **clean and healthy** animals.

Bring Your Pet Rabbit Home

Pet rabbits can be purchased from a pet store or adopted from an animal shelter. Be careful not to cuddle your rabbit too often, as this can make it sick.

Watch for changes in your rabbit's behavior and appearance, as these changes may indicate that something is wrong. Generally, a rabbit should be taken to the veterinarian once a year for a checkup, even if it is healthy.

Ask your veterinarian **which vaccinations your rabbit needs** to prevent common rabbit diseases.

Nose
A rabbit's nose twitches **20 to 120** times every minute.

Coat
A rabbit sheds its coat every **three months**.

Teeth
A rabbit's incisors grow up to **5 inches** each year.

RABBIT QUIZ

1

How many incisors and molars do rabbits have?

2

Why do rabbits with longer fur need to be brushed more often?

3

What are two of the most common rabbit species in North America?

4

What are male rabbits called?

5

What are female rabbits called?

6

How high can rabbits jump?

Answers

1. 6 incisors and 22 molars **2.** To prevent the fur from matting and to stop the rabbit from getting hairballs **3.** Cottontail and domestic rabbit **4.** Bucks **5.** Does **6.** About 3 feet (0.9 m) high

KEY WORDS

breeds: groups of animals that share specific characteristics

hazards: dangers

hind legs: the two rear legs of a four-legged animal

incisors: sharp teeth at the front of the mouth that are used for cutting

ingested: taken into the body by swallowing

molars: broad teeth at the back of the mouth that are used for grinding

receptors: sensitive nerve endings

regulate: control or maintain

temperaments: personalities

veterinarian: animal doctor

INDEX

Published by AV2
276 5th Avenue
Suite 704 #917
New York, NY 10001
Website: www.av2books.com

Library of Congress Cataloging-in-Publication Data

Names: Siemens, Jared, author.
Title: Rabbit / Jared Siemens.
Description: New York, NY : AV2, [2022] | Series: My favorite pet | Includes index. | Audience: Ages 8-11 | Audience: Grades 2-3
Identifiers: LCCN 2020053930 (print) | LCCN 2020053931 (ebook) | ISBN 9781791135126 (library binding) | ISBN 9781791135133 (paperback) | ISBN 9781791135140
Subjects: LCSH: Rabbits--Juvenile literature.
Classification: LCC SF453.2 .S56 2022 (print) | LCC SF453.2 (ebook) | DDC 636.932/2--dc23
LC record available at https://lccn.loc.gov/2020053930
LC ebook record available at https://lccn.loc.gov/2020053931

Printed in Guangzhou, China
1 2 3 4 5 6 7 8 9 0 25 24 23 22 21

012021
101120

Project Coordinator: Priyanka Das
Designer: Terry Paulhus

Photo Credits
Every reasonable effort has been made to trace ownership and to obtain permission to reprint copyright material. The publisher would be pleased to have any errors or omissions brought to its attention so that they may be corrected in subsequent printings.
AV2 acknowledges Getty Images as its primary image supplier for this title.